JOURNEYS ACROSS THE INVISIBLE BRIDGE

By Daniel Deng & Luka Kuol

Daniel Deng & Luka Kuol

Copyright © 2019 Detcro

ISBN-13: 978-1-7921-3718-1

Table of Contents

Acknowledgments

We would like to extend a special thanks to Jeffrey Campbell who has been instrumental to this project and many others over the years. His unique combination of technical understanding of the concepts under consideration, intellectual clarity and editorial competence make him a tremendous resource. His engagement with Francis Deng's ideas over the years make him, as a partner in Detcro Ltd., the right publisher for this project.

1. Introduction

This piece addressing the ideas of Ambassador Francis M. Deng, JSD, is co-written by two of his relatives, one a brother and the other a son. Rather than rely on a scholarly review of his published works, we take a more personal approach to trace the evolution of his thinking. Our purpose is to portray some of his most salient ideas in the context out of which they emerged, integrate them into what might be called his worldview, and root them back in the man behind those ideas. The reason for this approach is because we think the context and the man are also compelling dimensions of study that are valuable to record. Our interest is not biographical but to provide a nuanced perspective of Deng's ideas.

Deng was born in 1938 in Maker, the village of his maternal grandparents lying a few kilometers from his paternal village called Noong, and roughly 17 kms north of Abyei town in an area that is both a gulf and a bridge between what was then the two main regions of the Sudan, northern and the southern, now the two independent countries, Sudan and South Sudan. By the end of this exposition, this paradox of being both a gulf and a bridge will become clear, as will how responding to this and other tugs that often appear as polar opposites has shaped Deng's thinking. Over the course of five decades of scholarship, statesmanship and diplomacy, Deng's life has fundamentally been concerned with bridging boundaries and reconciling differences. In this paper, we argue that all of his ideas revolve around that fundamental core.

Deng's thinking can be understood by starting at the local level and progressing through the national, regional and global: locally, some of the concepts he paid particular attention to include Cieng,

Dheeng and Kooc e Nhoom (Dinka values that are nonetheless universal), the Invisible Bridge, Tradition and Modernization, and Development as Self-Enhancement from Within; nationally, they include Self-Determination as Self-Administration and the War of Visions, which dovetails with the New Sudan Vision; regionally, they include What Divides is What is Unsaid: Talking Things Out (African Principles for Managing Human Relations), and Constitutionalism; while globally they address Sovereignty as Responsibility, Foreign Policy as an Extension of Domestic Policy, Strategic Optimism, Constructive Management of Diversity and Idealism and Realism.

While Deng has served in the Cabinet of the United Nations, and therefore has had to apply his thinking to global mandates on such challenging issues as the human rights of Internally Displaced Persons and the prevention of genocide, all of his ideas are rooted at the local level; he developed his integral worldview based on the paradox of his home area of Abyei as both a gulf and a bridge whose differences require strategies for constructive management, along with values that he learned in his father's court and his mother's homestead. This paper is organized into five sections; other sections discuss how Deng's ideas germinated at the local level then progressed through the national, regional and global levels.

2. The Foundation of Deng's Ideas and Worldview

The Invisible Bridge

Earlier, we mentioned that Deng was born in a border area between what are now two independent countries, the republics of Sudan and South Sudan. This tug between two polar forces, one pulling southwards to Black Africa and the other pulling northwards to the Arab world, appears to have fostered within him a creative tension which he has sought to reconcile throughout his life. From this tension, he considered the fundamental concept of the Invisible Bridge. But, upon a closer read of the man and his works, this tension might well trace to an even more fundamental pull, due not to geographic location or political identification, but to the genetic poles of his maternal and paternal lines, or what scientists would refer to as mitochondrial and nuclear DNA. In Africa, these have always been approached in terms of ancestors and lineages, and are the subject of familial and tribal myths.

In Deng's search for personal identity, this first dissonance is due to the primordial fact of gender having separated man and woman and constitutes the first order of reconciliation in Deng's experience. His community, the Ngok Dinka of Abyei, operate according to a patrilineal agnatic descent system. This requires outward association with one's father and a more personal identification with one's mother. Indeed, throughout his life Deng dutifully cultivated this paternal identification, even authoring a biography of his father, *The Man Called Deng Majok: A Biography of Polygyny, Power and Change*. Inwardly, however, he deeply identified with his mother. This comes across clearly in his still unpublished memoirs – *Blood of Two Streams: Gender Balance in Parental Legacy*, which is a compilation piece to *The Invisible Bridge*, his educational memoirs. Although he has authored or contributed to over 40 books, these two manuscripts are still not available to the public.

The Man Called Deng Majok, first published in 1986 and republished in 1989, portrays Deng's legendary father, a tribal chief, as an iconic presence in his life. His relationship was ambivalent because the huge size of the family (the chief had over 200 wives and commensurately numerous children), the demands of chieftaincy, and the culture meant that despite in many ways being among the few privileged children with a closer relationship to his father than most of his brothers and sisters, there was nonetheless distance. Whereas he felt overwhelming love from his mother's side, his father's love was not as unconditional. Yet, his father's presence as an idea would shadow him across decades and continents. While his father epitomizes for Deng the just administrator who shrewdly dealt with internal and external relations of the tribe using a combination of diplomacy, force and compromise, Deng's maternal lineage draws from a spiritually-oriented line, known for their long vision and wisdom.

From this foundation of reconciling polar extremes across the boundary of man as an inherently gendered being, biologically and socio-culturally, Deng would in time speak about his ideas in terms of local, national, regional and global domains of experience and contribution. Of these, the local level is the most formative because it speaks to the deep influence his early upbringing had on his worldview. In essence, it is a worldview based on the integral logic of the Dinka village he came to know in Abyei, in his father's court where he witnessed the management of human relations, and in the home of his maternal relatives where he felt most fully loved.

Deng seems to reify this concept of the Dinka village and the court around which it was structured as an ideal for human development. In the ideal of tradition, Deng posits some of mankind's most noble virtues; however, it would be a mistake to take his promotion of the Dinka at face value. He does not hold any particular regard for the outer form of the tribe as a mark of belonging, but rather seeks to understand the internal logic that sustained a people for centuries in the absence of soldiers or militaries and that produced such remarkable personalities as his father and his mother, for whom he holds great admiration and respect.

In looking at the tribe, Deng sees a microcosm of social organization and cohesion in order to understand the complexities of human diversity and how these are best managed. His approach is to see what is good, focus on it and build upon it. This approach reconciles differences and bridges boundaries, and applies at all levels, from local to global.

Cieng, Dheeng and Kooc e Nhom

Deng writes extensively about three concepts, Cieng, Dheeng, and Kooc e Nhom, in his early works, *Tradition and Modernization* and *The Dinka of the Sudan*. Cieng refers to an ideal of human relations characterized by the search for harmony in unity while Dheeng refers to an ideal of proper conduct and physical presentation. Kooc e Nhom is normally associated with a form of immortality through the memory of the dead by the living and embraces genetic continuity of the individual and the species in general. It is the basis of the clan system, leads to veneration of the ancestors, and establishes the respect given to the aging process, including the parent/child relationship. For Deng, it is the bedrock of the entire system of values and institutions that constitute culture and continuity in change. Together, they frame a notion of human dignity that Deng considers both particular to the Dinka inasmuch as these concepts have context- specific connotations, but are also universal in their resonance with similar concepts everywhere. They are key to the idea of the bridging of boundaries and reconciling of differences because they set the benchmark, guidepost and final point of reference in the negotiation process when interests appear incompatible. Because they are universal, they are the constant referee, manifesting in a social context Deng has referred to as "the inner policeman," which he believes all people share – i.e. a sense of conscience.

For Deng, his image of a Dinka village seems to epitomize the idealized concept of human dignity as embedded in an integral set of social relations and values. What is also interesting is how he then takes the seminal notions born of that particular ideal

– Cieng, Dheeng and Kooc e Nhom – to the national, regional and international levels by virtue of the functional concept he refers to as the invisible bridge. In a very direct way, that bridge enabled him, no matter how far removed from his place of birth, to travel back, psychologically, to connect with those deeply personal attachments that root him. This would be important for Deng in his early years in Europe when he became disillusioned with the sense of isolation, and longed for the familiar sights, sounds, and relationships of home. The invisible bridge is therefore at once personal while also a mechanism for exploring the outside world and finding its universals.

Every human that travels away from home faces the threat of homesickness and has the possibility of using such an invisible bridge, through which they can stay rooted to their identity. The question, however, becomes personal: How fulfilling is that root? The answer depends on what that root represents to the person, how thoroughly they have understood it, and the place it occupies in the narrative of identity – definition of "self" – and an expectation for the world around them. Deng's invisible bridge does not take him to a place of ambivalence and doubt, but rather grounds him in safe place of comfort.

It is this grounding that is remarkably apparent in all of Deng's writings – no matter how theoretical the subject, when unraveled, his thinking draws its inner logic from the principles of Cieng, Dheeng, and Kooc e Nhom, which he recognizes as basically sacrosanct and universal. Even mundane aspects of village life, for example the household division of labor, construction techniques, and relationships to cattle, are infused with social and spiritual significance because of their expression of these foundational concepts not necessarily as something that has been actualized at any given time, but rather as the constant ideal

– the guidepost and the measure on life's roadmap. Throughout his career, Deng's reference to these concepts is unchanged and constant.

Tradition and Modernization

Deng wrote his first book on the basis of fieldwork he carried out in Abyei in the late 1950s when he was a student of law at Khartoum University. After he was diagnosed with glaucoma in London in 1962, he accelerated his writings starting by using that field research to author *Tradition and Modernization: A Challenge of Customary Law among the Dinka of the Sudan*. On June 9, 2016, at an award ceremony for the Glaucoma Foundation where he was being honored with the Kitty Carlisle Hart Award for Lifetime Achievement, Deng narrated the story about how his struggle with glaucoma pushed him to excel academically and deepen his academic endeavors that would consolidate his understanding about

Abyei and his own roots.

Now knowing that glaucoma posed the threat of blindness, I became depressed, concerned not only with the use of drops for life, but particularly about the dismal prospects for the future. To make things worse, I became suspected by the Government of the Sudan of masterminding and leading the Southern Sudanese opposition movement in Europe and was recalled back to the country.[1] Having been warned by well-informed sources in Khartoum about the certain

---

[1] As a member of the Law Faculty of the University of Khartoum, Deng had been granted a post-graduate fellowship to London University.

persecution I faced if I returned, I chose not to go.

After my second operation on the right eye, I asked my doctor what the prognosis for the future was, as I wanted to be realistic about the prospects. He told me that I would see as I did for three years and perhaps up to five years. Beyond that he couldn't tell. I concluded that I would probably be blind within five years. This, combined with my being in exile, meant that even if the political situation was resolved and I returned home, I would not be able to see my people.

Deng decided that whatever happened, he must make himself useful to society and he was racing against time. He therefore resolved to achieve as much as he could while he could still see. To compensate for not being able to see his people, he began to work on studies that would help connect with his background. Over the coming years, based on recordings he had made before leaving the country and continued to make after his return, he produced a number of materials on themes related to his Dinka background including songs, folk tales, ethnography of Dinka life cycle, oral history and cosmology, and the biography of his father, Deng Majok. He expedited his law studies to get his graduate degrees within the shortest possible period, obtaining his Masters and Doctorate in Law within three years from Yale University after graduating from Khartoum University. In the interim between Khartoum University and Yale Law, he had embarked on a post-graduate course in London which was disrupted by a combination of his eye crisis and political persecution – specifically he was accused by the Government of Sudan as masterminding and spearheading the early phases of the Southern Sudanese liberation movement. His idea in response to these personal crises was that having a doctorate would enhance his capacity to function, even without sight and irrespective of whether the authorities in Sudan allowed him back to his country or not. Fortunately, at precisely that point, he received a fellowship from Yale University in the United States to complete his graduate studies.

Deng's dissertation focused on the customary law of the Dinka and saw law in the context of their culture and the challenges of modernization in their society. Yale University Press published the dissertation, which was well received in the circles of African studies and was awarded the prestigious Herskovitz Award which was given to the best book published on Africa the year before. That book, *Tradition and*

Modernization: A Challenge of Customary Law among the Dinka, discussed the tension between forces of continuity and change in Dinka society. Deng proposed a notion of Transitional Integration as a response to the challenge. He conceived of it as a policy-oriented process of selecting the elements of continuity and those of change, and introducing changes purposefully and in a controlled manner so as to avoid the disruptions and losses that modernization might impose while also benefiting from all it had to offer.

Through the dissertation, together with Professors Lasswell and McDougal of the New Haven School of Jurisprudence, he created a framework that centered on Human Dignity as the overriding value proposition for human society. This made the particular study of the Dinka relevant to societies everywhere, who likewise, Deng surmised, pursue human dignity. Through the modality of family law, he was then able to apply the framework to the interview material he had amassed. The outcome was a thorough empirically-based exposé of his people during a period of intense changes. The Dinka come across as proudly assertive of their identity in the face of strong influences, both Arab-centered and European-centered, but also open to change, cognizant of the mixed opportunities for development and growth alongside threats of crisis and social disintegration. This book would lead Deng to embark on an ambitious attempt to pioneer a development project using Transitional Integration as its basic framework.

Development as Self-Enhancement from Within

In 1972, a peace agreement was signed in Addis Ababa that ended the first war, granted the southern Sudan regional autonomy, and gave Abyei the right to decide through a plebiscite whether to remain in the North or join the South. However, President Jaafar Mohamed

Nimeiri, who had signed the Addis Ababa Agreement, later refused to implement the provision on Abyei. Following his appointment as Ambassador shortly after the Addis Ababa Agreement, Deng proposed an alternative approach in a concept note that sought to turn Abyei from a contested area to a model of peace and unity by granting the Ngok Dinka 'mini autonomy' to be self-governing and provided with services and socio- economic development. He did this in the knowledge that Nimeiri would not implement the provision on Abyei and that the South was no longer prepared to go to war with the North over Abyei.

Deng's hope, as expressed in a piece he wrote regarding a reconciliation process between several of his brothers and the South Sudanese politician Bona Malual in 2017, was that "the people of the area would then see their position at the border as beneficial and play a bridging role between the North and the South as a peaceful meeting ground and a model for national unity and integration." With the blessing of the central government, Deng managed to convince Harvard Institute for International Development (HIID) to spearhead an integrated rural development project in Abyei; he also convinced the U.S. Agency for International Development (USAID) to fund it, with the idea that it would use the book *Tradition and Modernization* as a guide for applying an approach to development in the area based on Transitional Integration. As always, he was fiercely committed to the notion that differences, even those political differences over Abyei, could be reconciled.

Ever since that time, Deng has been a proponent of what he calls Development as a Process of Self-Enhancement from Within. The premise is that every human society has an integral set of values and institutions through which development takes place. Development itself as a notion of progress is problematic if it is seen as substituting for these out of a blind preference for imported alternatives. Without rootedness in the values and institutions that are endogenous to a society, externally driven development, no matter how appealing the imported elements appear in their original context, can only cause incoherence, disorientation and crisis. However, by seeing development as driven from within, the elements of continuity and change can serve to reinforce, strengthen and evolve the core identity of a people using the newly introduced elements as add-ons and complements, not substitutes. So for Deng, development requires a firm reckoning with the past to understand the present and build the future.

Furthermore, development as a process of self-enhancement from within requires harnessing the internal human resources of a people and directing those in continuation of the historical process. When understood in the context of Abyei, this meant utilizing the age set system through which boys and girls, and men and women, were systematically passed through stages of initiation and learning, organized to work according to societal requirements, and regimented into a fighting force to defend their community when needed. He saw this system as providing the basic social infrastructure for modern education and workforce development. Through its leaders, the age set system was directly connected to the Chieftaincy, which operated within the context of political and territorial units headed by Councils, chaired by chiefs, and culminating in the Paramount Chief, who symbolized the unity of the Ngok Dinka of Abyei and provided the community's top leadership. By building consensus from the bottom up through these structures, Deng recognized the tremendous power of community to mobilize its internal resources and set the course for its own development, whereby it could confidently choose new adaptations through Transitional Integration. Rwanda provides a good example of how home-grown solutions such as *Umuganda* (community work), *Ubwisungane* (mutual insurance), *Girinka* (a cow for every poor household) and *Agaciro* (self-worth or dignity similar to *Dheeng* in Dinka) are anchored to traditional values, institutions and age set to address human development, governance and service delivery. Deng saw that overriding values of Dinka society, such as the lineage concept of permanent identity and influence, Cieng and Dheng, could all be interpreted and applied to support the developmental strategy of transitional integration or self-enhancement from within.

The Harvard Project was challenging because the vision of development as self-enhancement from within that Deng believed in was so diametrically different than the standard approach to development where western experts are flown in for short periods of time to fix "problems," seen through the lens of western modernization, and import solutions based on their own experience. While this form of development did not seem to be working anywhere in the world, it was nonetheless and continues to be the frontline of foreign aid from the western world to the developing world, despite recognition of community-based processes, aid effectiveness and local ownership. Deng was frustrated as he saw his initiative result in business as usual in Abyei. HIID advocated the developmental concept of appropriate technology which Deng thought could have been in line with self enhancement from within, but which he believed they used rather negatively to limit financial external contributions instead of culturally contextualizing development. Nonetheless, he worked to bridge the differences with them regarding their approach to development, and together he and HIID eventually started seeing very positive results. In hindsight, he believes the Project was headed in the right direction but was ultimately undermined when, due to other agendas and misunderstandings on both sides, northern and southern, but particularly from among the Ngok Dinka and Missiriya elites and their respective local governments, conflict resumed, which ultimately engulfed northern and southern Sudan into another civil war in 1983.

3. Testing and Applying Deng's Ideas at a National Level

Self-Determination as Self-Administration

The HIID Abyei Project was an exercise in integrated rural development through local government. From it, Deng was attempting to address development as a process of self-enhancement from within using the community as a framework; however, why local government is considered the starting place is an important question that needs to be considered in understanding Deng's ideas. After all, Deng takes self-determination as the embodiment of all rights and the most proximal instrument, whether considered a legal right or a normative principle, to his ultimate goal of human dignity through the equitable shaping and sharing of values. So where, one might ask, does self-determination as a concept start? Saying it starts with local government assumes that the concept of "self" begins with government, and this is not consistent with Deng's wider worldview, which is rooted at a level that exists independent of the modern state. To explore his ideas on self-determination further, we believe it is necessary to go back across the invisible bridge to its anchor in his father's court and mother's homestead.

As an extension of the family concept, the African village that Deng's ideas circumscribe and project is a place where governance is naturally just, rational, and service-oriented, where relationships are integral and a people take care of each other. In this manner, the traditional system of governance symbolized by the African village is to Deng the best, achieving in the particular context of his own tribe and family, that governance across the world should strive to approximate. Modernization sees fully developed democracies as having evolved beyond rule by force, to enfold notions of equality, representation, rule of law and participation. And yet, these things have always existed in the African village, and, paradoxically, it is modernization that has thrust upon the village tumult and change, in the form of governments, their militaries, prisons and police – brute elements of power often exercised through local government administration.

Deng's ideas suggest that the dialectic of self-determination and unity emanate from the person within a family, a family within a community, a community within a country, a country within a region, so forth, right up until the point of a United Nations. Each unit also interacts directly with each other unit at each of the varying levels. At every level and for all conceivable relations, there are differences which may appear incompatible but hold the possibility for cooperation just as they do for conflict. The challenge posed by Deng is to promote cooperation at all the levels. Therefore, when he talks about self-determination through self-administration, local government becomes a strategic entry point, but the basis for self-administration does not begin there. In fact, the logical extension of his ideas takes us right back down to the family homestead and its relationship with the chief's court which traditionally is where things are discussed. From a policy standpoint, therefore, self-administration must start from the micro-economics of the household through all the degrees of local, regional and international integration. For Deng, this means globalizing while localizing.

Dynamics of Identification

Dynamics of identification have evolved from Deng's initially rather remote observations as a pioneering scholar of his own people to an effective model for understanding conflict and its transformation globally. While his ideas regarding the dynamics of identification support other normative principles, such as *Constructive Management of Diversity*, they find their own support in the Invisible Bridge concept which Deng used to navigate diversity in his own life. Dynamics of identification is also an expression of Deng's inclination to reconcile differences that may appear from one perspective as bi-polar opposites but are in fact polar complements. This is true of his maternal and paternal lineages, the competing communities of Ngok Dinka and Missiriya Arab along Sudan's North-South border, and the Black African community in which he was born and the White American community into which he ultimately married. His ideas in this regard are a contribution to wider humanism because they argue that while in the panorama of diverse races, ethnicities, religions, cultures and other orientations, an individual is enriched by his or her unique genealogy but shares in a humanity that is the unchanging anchor for an all-embracing universal identity in its multiplicity.

Francis Deng introduced the debate on identity as a factor in conflicts and nation-building in the Sudan in a study that was published in one of his shortest books, *Dynamics of Identification: A Basis for National Integration in the Sudan,* which Khartoum University Press published in 1973. Deng's thesis was that the evolution of the conflicting identities in the Sudan took place in a historical context in which converting to Islam, speaking Arabic, becoming culturally Arabized, and claiming descent from an Arab ancestry elevated one to a level of respect that sharply equated with being a Black African and a 'heathen', which made one a legitimate target for enslavement. Since Islam and Arabism encouraged such a liberal process of self-promotion, 'passing' became a well-documented trend among the indigenous populations of the North. Southern identity on the other hand evolved as one of resistance to Northern slave raids and Arab racial, cultural and religious hegemony.

The case of the Sudan demonstrates the fluidity and adaptability of identity and how it can be shaped and reshaped to serve the interest of the self-identifying character. Deng believed that with increasing recognition of diversity in pluralistic states and the stipulation of the human rights principle of non-discrimination, the myth of self-perception of Arabism would be adjusted to the reality of Sudanese admixture and its racial, ethnic, cultural and religious diversity in national unity. Deng's policy argument is that it is not the mere fact of identity differences that generates conflicts, but the way diversity is managed, which usually means that some groups enjoy the status of first-class citizens who enjoy the full rights of citizenship while other groups are discriminated, marginalized, excluded and denied the rights and dignity of citizenship.

Deng sees identity as both subjective, what people perceive themselves to be, and objective, what they really are by tangible criteria. Scholars emphasize subjectivity as what counts. Deng however argues that when subjective self-identification negatively impinges on the rights of others, it should be challenged. Identity can also be exclusive in a discriminatory way or inclusive in a way that accommodates others equitably.

Initially, Deng's ideas on identity conflicts were resisted in the Sudan and even internationally, including among scholars. In the Sudan, Northern elites saw the policy implication of his approach as challenging and threatening their 'Arabness', while Southern elites preferred to deal with the Northerners on the basis of their self-perception as Arabs. Ironically, *Dynamics of Identification* was misconstrued by some as advocating assimilation into the dominant identity of the North and by others as promoting the 'Africanization' of the North.

Internationally, there was also resistance to discussing identity as a factor in conflicts. This was in part a reaction to the racist policies of Nazi Germany in which nonscientific bases of differentiating races led to persecution of groups, the worst case being the Holocaust. Identity was also considered intangible as a factor and therefore not negotiable or susceptible to resolution. While Deng saw identity as central to the analysis of African conflicts in the African Studies Program at the Brookings Institution, and later in carrying out his UN mandates on internal displacement and genocide prevention, he initially met with strong resistance from his scholarly colleagues. It took persistent efforts to eventually turn them around.

Identity politics are now recognized as a significant factor in the contests for state power in Africa and across the world. But this recognition does not necessarily mean acceptance of diversity in unity and on equitable bases. In the United States of America, the Trump Administration is perceived to appeal to the "White Working Class", which is a new term only recently coined. Trump's alleged "Muslim Migration Ban" has been contested in courts across the country and reactions are acutely divided. In Europe, fears of migration are fueling nationalist movements. In the U.K., the British people voted with fear of migration to leave the European Union. Russia has aligned its foreign policy to support such nationalist movements in an effort to revive a sense of Pan-Eurasianism. Across Africa, the reality that tribal diversity remains the most persistent characteristic of the political landscape is unavoidable.

Deng articulated an important point regarding identity, which is still of an under-utilized utility in understanding the various types of identity politics across the world. While the center of gravity of an individual's identity is set in the objective genetic factors of lineage and tends to also be firmly rooted in a territory, citizenship and family, the outer perimeter of identity is not fixed, but rather is subjective and, therefore fluid and fungible. This perimeter can expand outward to include other groups or be permeable to align with other groups in the dynamic of identification. It can also retreat inward towards greater parochialism. It tends to retreat in times of certain types of shock and/or crises and expand in times of peace and/or security when fear, scarcity and desperation recede, and competition becomes zero-sum. Of global significance is the manner in which economic crises are now creating various forms of parochial identification, pitting groups against one another in a political discourse that tends towards aggression, antagonism and violence. Even more dangerous are those identities that define themselves in opposition to others. These may be the most insecure and reactionary in the shaping and sharing of power.

Deng would eventually admit that he had underestimated the depth and strength of Northern Sudanese commitment to Arabism and the related version of Islam. That was when he contributed to the formula of One Country, Two Systems as a means for reconciling conflicting visions of the North and the South for the Sudanese nation in a framework of unity in diversity. Even that compromise was not accepted in the end and the country was partitioned into two independent states.

Daniel Deng & Luka Kuol

War of Visions and the Vision of a New Sudan

In 1995, Deng wrote the book, *War of Visions: Conflict of Identities in the Sudan*. In it, he argued the war in the Sudan essentially reflected a crisis of national identity. He explained how the independence movement, pioneered and championed by the North and Egypt, the subordinate partner in the Anglo-Egyptian Condominium rule, was reluctantly supported by the South, which stipulated federalism and guarantees for the region as conditions for endorsing independence. Deng argues that on the basis of Northern promise that their concerns would be given "serious consideration" after independence, Southerners voted for independence. It soon became abundantly obvious that not only did the post-independence northern ruling elites dishonor their promise to the South, but worse, they despised diversity, and adopted Arabization and Islamization as policies for national unification through homogenization.

War of Visions explains how Southern reaction to the impending Arab domination first took the form of a mutiny by a battalion that soon escalated into a rebellion that resulted in the civil war which devastated the South for 17 years. That war, led by the Southern Sudan Liberation Movement (SSLM) and its Army, the Anyanya, aimed at the independence of the South from the North, but ended in a compromise solution that gave the South regional autonomy. The unilateral abrogation of that agreement in 1983 by President Nimeiri, who had made it possible in the first place, triggered the second civil war championed by the Sudan People's Liberation Movement and Sudan People's Liberation Army (SPLM/SPLA). Unlike the first liberation movement, which called for Southern secession, the SPLM/SPLA postulated the creation of a New Sudan that would be free from any discrimination based on race, ethnicity, religion, culture, or gender.

The vision of the New Sudan was mainly that of Dr. John Garang de Mabior, Chairman of the SPLM and Commander-in-Chief of the SPLA. Initially, it was not understood, far less supported in the North and the South, even within his movement. The fighting men and women in the South took it as a clever ploy to allay the fears of those opposed to separation within the country, in the African region, and in the international community. Deng believes that while Garang was talking the language of the New United Sudan, Southerners were fighting for the secession of the South from the North. In discussing the New Sudan vision, Deng would say at a symposium at the Center for Conflict Resolution in Cape Town:

What is important to
underscore in the context of

Garang's vision for a New United Sudan is that the dichotomy between the Arab-Islamic North and the African South is largely a fiction. While the North has been labeled Arab, even those who can trace their genealogy to Arab origins are a hybrid of Arab and African race, and even their culture is an Afro-Arab race...The vision of the New Sudan therefore promises to liberate all these people, along with the South, from their marginalization, and to create a country of genuine pluralism and equality, with a greater influence for the previously marginalized African groups. An aspect of Africanization therefore underlay the vision.

The New Sudan vision was largely in line with Deng's thesis regarding the identity conflict in Sudan. He argued that two sets of normative issues underlie the North-South conflict: "Failure to manage constructively the racial, ethnic, religious and cultural diversities of the country and, correlatively, failure to build on the indigenous cultures, values and institutions, which were deemed primitive and inferior to the Arab-Islamic culture, postulated as the national framework for unity and nation-building." While right up until the signing of the Comprehensive Peace Agreement (CPA) in 2005 and beyond, many continued to perceive the War of Visions as simplistically a North-South issue; Deng early on recognized that the national challenge penetrated deep into the North. He recognized that the CPA "addresses this multilayered crisis of identity by giving the South the right of self-determination, to decide whether to remain within a united Sudan or become fully independent, through a referendum to be exercised after a 6-year interim period, while, at the same time challenging the North and all those who want to see the Sudan united, including African countries, the West, the Arab World, and others, to exert all efforts to make unity an attractive option for the South." He had helped to coin the concept of "making unity attractive," and also the formula of "one Sudan, two systems." In fact, both of these were largely his conceptual inventions, which helped to frame the CPA. And while most southerners saw the CPA as a means towards southern independence, Deng fundamentally believes in the New Sudan.

Deng recognized that "the South will have its own government, fully independent of Northern interference, its own army, virtually at par with the national army, its own branch of the National Bank, which, unlike its Northern counter-part branch that will remain Islamic, will be conventional." He also recognized that "despite a national foreign policy, the South will have the right to establish bilateral relations with international trade and development partners" with "an effective role in the Government of National Unity (GNU)." Yet, he was not sure as to what the South would do with it. He hoped that "What is likely to emerge is a restructured Sudan in which the traditionally dominant Arab-Islamic center will cede power to the periphery and by the same token allow the process of African renaissance to bloom." He further hoped that the arrangement would provide "the South with the opportunity to manage its own internal ethnic diversity, but also to orientate its system of governance to its indigenous values and institutions through a strategy of transition integration that bridges tradition with modernity in dynamic synergy." These were the best case-scenarios.

Deng did question however, "Whether the Government of the South will, in fact do this," concluding rather that it "will remain to be seen," particularly "without Dr. John Garang de Mabior, who was a major force in its (the CPA's) achievement and the prospects of its successful implementation." He questioned as well whether the national government would make the unity of Sudan attractive to the people of Southern Sudan.

His 2016 book, *Bound by Conflict: Dilemmas of the Two Sudan*, largely answers the question with the power of hindsight. No, the CPA has not led to the transformation of the South, nor had the North allowed an African renaissance to create diversity within unity in the areas still under its control. Rather, both Sudan and South Sudan continued to replicate the systems of deprivation that led to the history of war. The South Sudan had lost sight of the ideals of its own liberation and was locked in a complex dynamic with the Sudan, where each accused the other of supporting rebel movements, both were determined to consolidate power by military means, and neither had launched the type of inclusive development that Deng advocated for as a process of self-enhancement from within. The War of Visions had taken root in the South; although devoid of religious dimensions, nonetheless remains a conflict of identities and a challenge of diversity management requiring a bridging of differences that had become gulfs separating tribes in a terrible struggle for the central seat of power.

What divides is what is unsaid: Talking Things Out

Deng has been known widely for coining the term "what divides is what is unsaid", which Dr. John Garang quoted in his popular letter in February 2000 to former prime minister of Sudan, Sadig al-Mahdi. Deng sees negotiation and the closely related field of diplomacy as essentially management of human relations involving individuals, groups, or nations. While accepting that "grounds for conflict exist in normal human relations," he believes "people are more apt to cooperate and harmonize their incompatible or potentially conflictual positions, and that conflict is in fact a crisis that signifies a breakdown in the normal pattern of behavior." His original grounding in Abyei taught him that there is a normative code, with the normal pattern one of relative cooperation and mutual accommodation, even in a competitive framework. In his view, "To call that state one of conflict would be to put a negative value judgment on positive motivations and endeavors," and to ignore what he believes is a relatively high degree of success in peaceful interaction. He therefore argues that through education, both formal and informal, desirable norms of behavior can be promoted and, therefore, he pointed out certain principles that might be promoted in such a way as to assist in "reconciling, harmonizing, or managing incompatible interests by fostering a process of institutionalized peaceful interaction."

According to Deng, the following principles "derive from personal experiences and are rooted in values, norms, and mores that emanate from a specific African family and cultural background among the Dinka of Sudan". Although personal and rooted in the Dinka, Sudanese, and African cultural contexts, they represent values that can claim universal validity, despite cross-cultural variations on the details and their applicability."

> Principle One: Rights and wrongs, though seldom equal, are rarely one-sided. Even when you feel sure that you are in the right,

you must not only strive to fit yourself into the shoes of the other side but must make the other side recognize that you are genuinely interested in his or her point of view.

Principle Two: It is unhealthy to keep grievances "in stomach" or "in heart." Talking it out, the title of a book I wrote on the theme, is not only the best way to resolve differences or grievances, but it also essential for one's mental and even physical health. Often "what is not said is what divides," to use the words of an article I wrote on that theme.

Principle Three: Face-saving is crucial to resolving conflicts. One must avoid saying anything that is humiliating to the other side, and where possible, it is advisable to show deference, even to an adversary, provided it is not cheap flattery.

Principle Four: It is important to listen very carefully and allow the other party to say all that she or he considers significant or relevant. Resolving differences is not a game of wits or cleverness, but of addressing the genuine concerns of the parties in conflict. In Dinka folktales, the cleverness of the fox eventually turns against the fox. Ideally, resolutions must have an element of give and take, although the distribution should be proportional to the equations of the rights and wrongs involved. In assessing the outcome of a negotiated settlement of a dispute, it is unwise to boast of victory, for that implies defeat for the other side and therefore an unsatisfactory outcome.

Principle Five: Historical memory of relations gives depth to the perspectives of the parties involved and the issues involved, but one must avoid aggravating the situation with negative recollections and emphases and should instead reinforce constructive dialogue with the positive recollections or interpretations of events without distorting the facts.

Principle Six: The mediator must be seen as impartial, but where there is reason to believe that he or she is closer to one side in any capacity, the mediator must reach out to the more distant party. However, this must not be at the cost of fairness to the party close to the mediator. Impartiality does not mean having no the issues in dispute, even though voicing opinions should be carefully coached to maximize the bridging roles and promote mutual understanding.

Principle Seven: The mediator must listen very patiently to both parties, and even when there are flaws in what is said, the mediator must appear to give due weight to each party's point of view. The popular view that the indigenous African system of dispute settlement, where people sat under the tree and talked, until they reached a consensus, reflects a broadly shared African normative behavior. Where explaining the opponent's view on a specific issue might facilitate the bridging process, the mediator should intercede to offer an explanation as part of consensus building.

Principle Eight: While the wisdom of word and ability to persuade are important, leverage is pivotal. This means that the mediator must have or be believed to have the ability to support the process with incentives or threat of negative consequences, according to the equations of responsibility for the success or failure of the negotiations. In the past among the Dinka, spiritual powers of divine leadership provided the required leverage. In the modern context, influencing the balance of power to create a "mutually hurting stalemate" and help to advance the process of "ripening for resolution", to borrow the famous words of renowned scholar of conflict analysis William Zartman, is part of the leverage that can effectively facilitate the mediator's task.

Principle Nine: Diplomatic negotiations combine elements of both interpersonal relations and third-party mediation in the negotiator representing his/her government, and in a sense combine negotiating with mediating between the respective governments involved. Discretion and creativity in adapting the official position to dynamics of the situation with a degree of flexibility is critical to the prospects of successful bridging.

Principle Ten: While the tendency of negotiators is to see the outcome of their efforts in terms of winning or losing, especially for domestic consumption the desired outcome should be one in which neither side sees itself as a total winner or loser except where the rights and wrongs involved are incontrovertibly clear. The win-win formula should be the objective, and whatever the equations of winning or losing in the mediated or negotiated outcome, as noted in Principle Four, neither side should boast about winning and by implication humiliate the other side as a loser. There must be a degree of parity in both sides winning or losing.

Constitutionalism

As Sudan's Minister of Foreign Affairs, Deng engaged extensively with African Governments. Later, as Director of the Africa Project at the Brookings Institution, he continued to explore the root causes of the governance crisis in Africa. His research led him to two sets of interrelated issues: the management of diversities through various forms of self-administration, including self-determination as a model of governance; and cultural contextualization through the application of relevant indigenous norms within the framework of constitutionalism. In this notion of constitutionalism, he stressed democratic principles of consensual decision-making, the pursuit of human dignity through culturally relevant principles of "human and people's rights," and socio-economic development as a process of self-enhancement from within that balances growth with equitable distribution. For him:

> Constitutionalism is
> governed by fundamental
> concepts that set the rules
> for participating in the
> shaping and sharing of
> values. It should be seen as
> a living process that is
> constantly evolving with the
> participation of its people to
> promote their ownership of
> governing frameworks.

While constitutionalism has conventionally been understood to constrain the use and abuse of power by the state to promote fundamental rights and freedoms and maintain the rule of law, increasingly it is being viewed as emphasizing the promotion of human dignity.

4. Deng's Global Ideas and Worldview

Sovereignty as Responsibility

Deng served as Representative of the Secretaries-General, Boutros Ghali and Kofi Annan, on Internally Displaced Persons (IDPs), and then for Ban ki-Moon as Special Advisor on Genocide Prevention. His work on behalf of these leaders of the UN over the course of two decades introduced him to countries in conflict which are so acutely divided that he wondered how they would ever become united as nations. On his dozens of missions to affected countries, he would first meet with the leadership and then visit the IDPs. He would ask the IDPs what message they wanted him to convey to their national leaders. Their responses were almost identical, wherever he went. They did not see those in government as their leaders because they did not identify with the state, nor did they feel the state signified them as part of the nation. "To those rulers, we are not citizens, but criminals, and our only crime is our poverty," one community leader in a Latin American country responded; "none of our people is in that government," a spokesman in a Central Asian country replied. In an African country, the Prime Minister said, "The food you give to those people (his country's IDPs) is killing my soldiers."

Deng understood these reactions to indicate acutely divided societies where large elements of the nation, which might even historically have been nations on their own, do not feel connected to the state. In fact, these more natural communities see the state as their enemy and are seen as enemies of the state. Deng was faced with a rather impossible situation by representing the UN in trying to engage with Member States who wield the shield of sovereignty against external scrutiny of their internal conflicts. These conflicts were sensitive, politicized, and violent. Why would they want to cooperate with the international community, particularly when they were being accused of mass atrocities, and sometimes genocide? For them, the more logical strategy may often be to use sovereignty as a shield to scare off critics, hiding behind projected nationalism and entrenching the regime; and yet, Deng believed that any differences, no matter how incompatible the interests appear, may be bridged.

So, he put the onus back on the host governments by proposing that the challenge of identity conflicts is in how to manage diversity constructively to promote a sense of equality, belonging on equal footing, and pride in being a citizen who enjoys the dignity and rights associated with citizenship. He would point out, subtly, that this is an objective which no self-respecting government can question, far less oppose. This formulation provided a positive basis of engagement with governments during the time of his UN mandates. It was the origin of a concept that he developed and referred to as 'Sovereignty as Responsibility.' The 'Guiding Principles on Internal Displacement', which he developed with renowned international legal experts and presented to the United Nations Commission on Human Rights in 1998 as a normative basis for preventing internal displacement and providing protection and assistance to the internally displaced during and after displacement were based on stipulating sovereignty as Responsibility with international assistance as needed.

Sovereignty as Responsibility was later reformulated as the Responsibility to Protect (R-to-P), which is now considered an important mechanism for the UN Security Council's activities in states considered to be failing their people. But there is a tendency among states to see R-to-P as posing a threat of international intervention and it is therefore resisted, while sovereignty is viewed as emphasizing the responsibility of the state for its people and is therefore more acceptable.

Foreign Policy is an Extension of Domestic Policy

The other difference that Deng bridges is between domestic and foreign policy, which is a variant of the tension surrounding the issue of sovereignty. The way he approaches foreign policy is to see it as an extension of domestic policy, by which he means that in order to have a strong foreign policy, a country must have a good domestic commodity to represent. Such a commodity is achieved through domestic policy agenda, which equips the diplomatic corps, through the foreign ministry with the necessary tools for constructive engagement with the international community. However, no matter how eloquent and skilled a country's diplomats may be, they cannot put a good face on a bad commodity.

When Deng accepted the responsibility of being the first Permanent Representative to the United Nations on behalf of South Sudan, he did so on the basis of a strategy document that he circulated across the Foreign Ministry and within the Presidency which explicitly stated his view of foreign policy. The implication was to put the onus on the Government as a whole, including the President himself, to originate foreign policy in good domestic policy. Given his moral rooting in concepts of Cieng and Dheeng, it would not have been possible for Deng to promote a country whose policies he did not agree with. With the political conflict that was soon to engulf the country and the terrible massacres that were to be committed by Government and Opposition forces, this role of representing South Sudan would become increasingly difficult to justify. Perhaps it was to his fortune that he was recalled to South Sudan. Upon returning to Juba, the President appointed him as a Roving Ambassador and a member of the Leadership of the National Dialogue.

The National Dialogue was to become the good domestic commodity that Deng could represent internationally. In many ways, it was a forum for Talking Things Out, and it allowed him to revive his focus on the African principles for managing human relations. The art of bridging differences would be fully required if the National Dialogue was to have any positive impacts on the country, whose economy had collapsed, army had splintered and state institutions were failing. Deng tirelessly thrust himself into the work of the National Dialogue, soon emerging as a pivotal force that despite the extreme skepticism and even cynicism of the international community and much of the domestic constituency alike, forged ahead. In many ways, it seemed that without the integrity of the leadership colleagues, the National Dialogue would have been dismissed as a front for tribalism and perpetuation of the status quo. But Deng and his colleagues insisted on the principles of inclusivity, credibility and transparency, ensuring that not only would the National Dialogue reach out to all parties, even those carrying arms, but that it would go down to the grassroots level.

Strategic Optimism, Opportunity in Crisis and Constructive Engagement

Part of the reason Deng was able to accept the responsibility of leadership within the South Sudan National Dialogue, despite the high likelihood of its failure, is his belief in another idea, which he calls strategic optimism. This concept states that optimism opens doors while pessimism leads to a dead end. Therefore, if one is to achieve anything in life, optimism is of great strategic value whereas pessimism is self-defeating. Oftentimes Deng, at various levels of his engagement, would bemoan the prophets of doom, and challenge them with the words of Nelson Mandela: At a small dinner Deng attended, he said that in every person, by virtue of their humanity, there is some good. Deng always looks to reach that higher angel in a person and build from there. In engaging the international community on the National Dialogue, which they were reluctant to support, he challenged them with the same message: When looking at South Sudan's leaders, they should not reduce them to the terrible acts committed under their watch, but appeal to their higher angels on the basis of a shared commitment to improving situations.

As he often said, Deng did not believe that a leader can accept for his people to suffer and remain comfortable in their misery; and surely, no foreigner can assume to want peace and stability in a country more than the people of that country. On that basis, Deng against all odds was an evangelist of constructive engagement, believing that the main issue was to identify the problems and build capacities for peace. Yet, those who know his thinking also realize that this was not in opposition to the concept of a peaceful process of lawful regime change because Deng also knew that for South Sudan to proceed beyond its collapse, there would need to be a peaceful transfer of power, albeit with degrees of continuity and a soft landing that would ensure the dignity of the departing leader through assurances of his physical and material security and the security of his assets and legacy. In that way, the leader could be assured that they would continue to be seen as leader, even after Government involvement. At the Award ceremony mentioned earlier, Deng said,

The two themes of my
experience with glaucoma
lead to two major
conclusions. First, I believe
in strategic optimism and
maintain a profound
conviction that pessimism
leads to a dead end while
optimism, provided it is not
fool-hardy, opens doors for
constructive endeavors and
achievement. Second, I
believe that in crises often
lie opportunities which offer
prospects for
compensation. With these
two themes in my response
to glaucoma and the fact
that I can still see today, I
feel that glaucoma has not
necessarily been a curse,
but a challenge that
motivated me to do things

that I might not have done otherwise.

In seeking the opportunity in crisis, it is true that Deng always seemed to prefer the conciliatory approach. This could be seen by some who doubt the sincerity of leaders and realize that just as humans have higher angels, they also have lower selves, where demons dwell. Indeed, there have been leaders for whom history accords no great narrative of redemption but rather a story of their diabolical deeds and tragic deaths. No one, for example, cried over the unceremonious fall of Mobutu Sese Seko, who held Zaire in a death grip for over 30 years. The tendency for people to believe enforcement of the rule of law is the quickest and surest path to justice is the reason why Sovereignty as Responsibility was quickly reinterpreted as the Responsibility to Protect, placing the onus on the international community to use the tools at its disposal to demand of governments that they respect the human rights of their people. Deng, however, was not blindly committed to conciliation. As a matter of principle, he recognized the validity of the use of sanction, criminal courts and even military intervention, although he questioned the credibility of their practical application. In fact, his time in the UN made him realize that seldom does the international community have a unified position from which to act, or a clear policy for how to impose a regime change. If they did, and conditions were right, he would have certainly opted for the most pragmatic course towards replacing rogue governments, but the reality he observed at the UN during his two decades within the UN cabinet was that the United Nations was actually an organization of divided nations, within and among themselves. Hence, the sticks never seemed to work, and most rhetoric was sound-and-fury signifying very little.

Constructive Management of Diversity

Deng points out that diversity is a global phenomenon. Hardly any country can claim to be fully homogeneous. So, diversity is pervasive, yet not all countries characterized by diversity experience such terrible identity conflicts. Some manage well while others do not do so well, and yet others perform dismally. The difference begins with their notion of sovereignty, whether leaders have accepted it as a responsibility or still use it as a shield. The states that see sovereignty as a responsibility are more likely to be pursuing inclusive development for their people, while those that use it as a shield are more likely to be engaging in zero-sum power struggles. Many are caught in the transition area between these two different systems and the rules they imply.

The paradox, however, is that the system of governance he grew up experiencing, and ultimately idealizing, was partly democratic and partly autocratic, and based on the relationship between an inherited chieftaincy and the colonial rulers. His deeply personal connection to this system of governance, personified in his father, the legendary Paramount Chief of the Ngok Dinka, Deng Majok, forms a thread that is woven through his thinking across disciplines and levels of service; it forms an inclusive platform on which he contends, intellectually, with the traditional village, and the modern colonial state. The autochthonous segmentary lineage-based system of self-administering clans and self-reliant homesteads meant that the autocratic system of governance of Ngok Dinka society was in no way akin to the military autocracy of Europe but was something totally different – a place where rule was generally based on the will of the people, without which legitimacy to rule could never be imposed by force. This led him to often say, "our people are inherently democratic, but that makes them hard to govern." It also problematizes the notion of democracy. If people are self-reliant and self-administering, then are they not self-determining? And isn't self-determination the end result that democracy seeks to accomplish? In Deng, we therefore can see an embrace of the democratic ideal as well as a simultaneous sublimation of the concept itself within others, which for him are of a higher, more explicit, and therefore, meaningful order — sovereignty, dignity, self-determination, and constitutionalism to name just a few. With these, the question of whether to have elections or not seems less straightforward.

At a national level, the fierce pride in his people and the recognition that in the village Cieng and Dheeng define standards, whether individual or collective, his threads of thought were woven into the New Sudan vision which he, along with John Garang, articulated. He defined the New Sudan as a place free from discrimination, where all groups, regardless of how small, would feel a part of the nation and be accorded a fair share of control over their lives and destinies without interference from the center. With such a system in place, he believes the greater power of unity would prevail, and no group would seek secession because deprivations would be eliminated and privileges would be merit-based. In the New Sudan vision, we do not get a simplistic notion of democracy as evidenced by elections, or even "civil society," but a more basic question as to whether people – and specifically families in homesteads who are part of nations within nations – feel that they are in control of their own lives and destinies, not theoretically, but practically, administering their own resources and directing the course of their own development from within the socio-cultural infrastructures they inherited from their ancestors.

For the Sudan, Deng genuinely believed in the possibility of unity on the basis of equality and envisioned the African culture he had experienced growing up, in contrast to the Christian and Muslim emphasis on exclusivity of religious beliefs, as being accommodating enough to accord everyone their dignity. In that sense, he saw Sudan as primarily an African nation, but one in which Arabs, like any other "tribe," would be free to participate and contribute. His New Sudan vision was close to Garang's, perhaps only with a difference in emphases. It was through the modality of this shared vision that the two became friends, and it was that friendship, rooted in that shared vision, that propelled Deng to help build a U.S. constituency for the Sudan People's Liberation Movement (SPLM).

For him, that work was an expression of the Invisible Bridge. While many of his brothers had taken to the bush to fight a liberation war against the Government in Khartoum, he had opted to pick up the pen and lived in the U.S., where he used his various fellowships and appointments with policy institutes to push the agenda of the liberation struggle not as a member of a political party, but as a nationalist committed to certain ideals. Under the Center for Strategic International Studies (CSIS), he coined the concept of One Sudan, Two Systems that eventually became the backbone of the CPA. Perhaps now he would modify that to be One Sudan, Multiple Systems, to encompass the other marginalized groups left behind with the independence of South Sudan. At that time, however, the core agreement needed seemed to be between the SPLM and the Government in Khartoum, and it was a formula, which by making unity attractive, was meant to safeguard the unity of the country.

Idealism with Realism

When Deng was appointed in 2007 by the UN Secretary General as Special Adviser on the Prevention of Genocide, he struggled with how to reconcile his aspiring task of genocide prevention and the practical challenge of how to not only negotiate sovereignty but also engage governments in a constructive dialogue on issues of sovereignty and responsibility, good governance and equitable management of diversity. In 2010, Deng shared the dilemma of his mandate in a published piece called *Idealism and Realism Negotiating: Sovereignty in Divided Nations*, which was actually the text of the 2010 Dag Hammarskjöld Lecture, organized by the Dag Hammarskjöld Foundation and Uppsala University. In his comments, we see the visionary thinking of a man of ideas, but we also see the pragmatism of a man who has had to apply his ideas in order to achieve results in a real world of complex challenges.

> ... the delicate balance between asserting the need for international protection for the vulnerable and the need for constructive engagement on the part of governments seems to be working. I know that this is not the approach favored by those who believe that on these matters we should cry out loud, stand on the mountain-top and preach what is right and condemn what is wrong. However, when we do that, we might satisfy our conscience, but how much can we help the people who need to be helped in a practical way?

5. Rooting Deng's Ideas back to the Stabilization of Abyei

Stabilization of Abyei Area

In March 2014, Deng presented to the United Nations Security Council a Proposal for the Interim Stabilization of the Abyei area. In it, he made the case for meeting the pressing needs of the Ngok Dinka and their neighboring communities to the North and South, in particular the Missiriya Arabs, who traverse the area in the dry season in search of water sources and grazing lands. He also addressed the political sensitivities over the future status of Abyei between Sudan and South Sudan, and the strategic importance of considering and alleviating the legitimate concerns of the Government of the Sudan, Government of South Sudan and the neighboring ethnic communities to the North and the South in order to foster an inclusive cooperative approach to the normalization and socio-economic development of the area in the interest not only of the neighboring communities, but also of the two countries. It came at a time when the people of Abyei conducted their community referendum with its outcome not recognized by governments of South Sudan or Sudan, African Union or United Nations.

His starting point was that as a result of the stalemate over the political status of Abyei between Sudan and South Sudan, the Ngok Dinka, who are the indigenous population of the area, have been abandoned in a vacuum of virtual statelessness without the responsibility for protection and assistance that is normally associated with the rights of citizenship. This has changed an area that has historically been a constructive bridge on which the neighboring communities of the North and the South of the then Sudan met, co-existed and interacted peacefully and cooperatively despite their racial, ethnic, religious and cultural differences into a battleground of violently devastating conflict between the neighboring communities and the now independent countries of Sudan and South Sudan. The Ngok Dinka, who have been the primary victims of this tragic development, cry out for international rescue operation to protect them and assist them in resuming their normal life and generating a self-sustaining process of socio-economic development.

Deng went on to argue that the United Nations Interim Security Force in Abyei (UNISFA) is providing a much-appreciated level of protection, and the Government of South Sudan is supporting a semblance of badly needed administrative presence in the area. However, the people of Abyei are now totally dependent on the international community for humanitarian assistance and the very limited infrastructural and socio-economic development activities they have. In addition, they have been denied the 2% of oil revenues promised to them since 2005 from the oil produced in the area.

Even the protection provided by UNISFA is restricted to a small fraction of Ngok Dinka territory. Most of the traditional home areas to which the Ngok would like to return remain without protection. He told the UN Security Council that UNISFA cannot provide protection where there are no people, but people cannot settle where there is no protection. This creates the dilemma of which one should come first, protection or settlement. The ideal is that both should occur simultaneously, particularly because the people intend to return. The questions are will they be protected, and who will provide them basic services?

The gist of the proposal is that the

area desperately needs a more comprehensive and effective program of service delivery and socio-economic development that builds on the social and cultural values of the people, their institutional structures, and their traditional operational patterns. The plan is to adopt a strategy of transitional integration that makes effective use of the local resources and resourcefulness while it also approaches development as a process of self enhancement from within, thus combining self-reliance with well-targeted complementary international support.

For this to be acceptable to key stakeholders and therefore operationally feasible, he argued that it must foster peace and security in the wider area by addressing the pressing needs not only of the Ngok Dinka inhabitants, but also those of the neighboring communities in the region, specially the nomadic Missiriya Arabs who enter the area during the dry season in search of water and pastures for their livestock. Like the Ngok Dinka, the Missiriya also have pressing needs for service delivery and socio-economic development in their own areas of normal residence and needs for health and educational services as well as care for their livestock along their seasonal migration routes in the Ngok Dinka area and further into South Sudan.

Deng argued that assessing the needs of the Missiriya, both in their home areas and during their seasonal migration, needs to be carried out by those familiar with their conditions. The preparedness of the international community to assist in meeting their needs should also be made evident early to respond to the requirements of all communities in the region. However, this should not be a reason to delay the stabilization program.

Deng's calculus is that the ripple effects of meeting the needs of these neighboring border communities should contribute toward improving bilateral relations between Sudan and South Sudan and return the area to play its historic role as a constructive North-South bridge in the Old Sudan and a conciliatory point of contact and interaction between the racial, ethnic, cultural and religious diversities of the country, now region.

The Proposed Stabilization Agenda should therefore operate on the dual track of meeting the needs of the communities in the region while also engaging the two Governments of Sudan and South Sudan to cooperate with the international community in the delivery of essential services and support for the socio-economic development of the area. This would not only be in the interest of their respective communities in the region, but also in the long-term mutual interest of both countries.

Deng went on to share this proposal

with the Governments of both Sudan and South Sudan as well as with African Union leaders concerned with the relations between the two countries. The positive response of both governments to this appeal to their responsibility as sovereigns helped to change the zero-sum calculus between them for the first time in decades. This initiative of Deng was described by UN Secretary General Special Envoy for South Sudan and Sudan as a major diplomatic breakthrough that allows the two governments to engage again on Abyei. They seemed to respond well to the idea of building a common ground and serving the mutual interests of all the stakeholders as well as addressing all legitimate concerns over the area. He made a strong case that meeting the needs of the neighboring communities in the area should not be held hostage by the political differences of the leaders in their respective capitals. At the same time, he made an equally convincing positive case that stabilizing the area is a means of breaking the impasse over Abyei and therefore a way out of the quagmire facing these leaders about the future status of the area.

Deng's current work on the stabilization of Abyei demonstrates that he understands that it is easier to be idealist than realist as the later requires hard choices. These difficulties notwithstanding, Deng reminds us that we can all be dreamers but not all of us can match those dreams with the pragmatic actions of a realist who must operate in a world of nuance. The current case of Abyei is a good case to test these two concepts. While the vast majority of the people of Abyei recognize and appreciate the tireless efforts that Dr. Deng has exerted to shift the zero-sum calculus of the two antagonistic governments and make them see the mutual gain to be had from their cooperation over Abyei, those people who are less realist and more idealist tend to be more dismissive.

Idealists on the Abyei issue believe that the focus should exclusively lie with achieving the outcome of community referendum and final status of Abyei, and they argue that the initiative of Dr. Francis Deng may not help in realizing such a pure ideal. Others, mostly resettled far away from the area and participating through internet, stress that what we want is freedom at any cost, and not development. One even went as far as to say any reference to internally displaced persons in the stabilization initiative was an acceptance that people of Abyei are citizens of Sudan. This argument of course ignores the fact that the people of Abyei were displaced to South Sudan in 2008 and 2011 and not to Sudan. More importantly, some of these idealists have already achieved their freedom in the Diaspora where they have benefited from educational opportunity and all the goods and services of a developed nation. These same idealists argue that the people of Abyei must sit and wait for such a freedom to be delivered to them from the government in Juba alone, despite its current challenges on other fronts with the impacts of civil war and the relative leverage of Khartoum, particularly given their possession of the oil pipeline. If they were to acknowledge such real-world considerations, the idealist would have to come down to earth.

Realists on the other hand support the initiative of Dr. Francis Deng but they maintain that such initiative for stabilization of the area through mutual cooperation of the two governments in support of similar cooperation among neighboring tribes at a local level should not undermine the ideal of the final status of Abyei. They argue that the current status quo in Abyei is so appalling that if it continues, people may desert the area and leave to Sudan. They argue, as does Dr. Deng, that while waiting for the final status, efforts must be exerted to provide basic services and assist the return of displaced persons to their home areas with dignity, lest the area be lost for good. They assert that while they have made their decision to be part of South Sudan unequivocally clear and there is nothing that will change that outcome, those facts should not deprive the area's people of the services and development they desperately need, including access to their share of oil revenues which has been denied them due to the political impasse.

In review of the various positions on the issue of Abyei's stabilization, idealists seem to fear taking initiatives because they try by all means to avoid blame; and yet, review of these same positions reveal how the idealists seem to enjoy criticizing any initiative without the burden of providing reasonable alternatives. In responding to idealists, who were critical in their faraway comfort zones, of SPLM during the liberation struggle, Dr. John Garang used to tell them (idealists) that we (realists) are not perfect but at least we are doing something through liberation to change what is happening in Sudan; but for you (idealists), we will not expend the energy to criticize you because you are doing nothing to be criticized. Realists are more likely to be criticized than idealists.

Deng through his efforts at local, national and regional levels shows that it is important to combine both idealism and realism as they complement each other. Being realist without ideals may take you nowhere as you would lack the sense of direction that comes from having a vision of your destination; and being idealist without realism would take you nowhere also as you would just contemplate "pie in the sky". Combining the two concepts has been indispensable for Deng in navigating his journey in life and is a core competence of a bridge builder. It could indeed be argued that the principles of a New Sudan or any normative framework that manages diversity constructively on the basis of full equality in unity, and peace, reconciliation and cooperation among diverse groups is more idealistic than separation based on ethnic differences. However, translating that into meaningful outcomes takes a determination to act in a world where the consequences of our decisions, as individuals and nations, are all very real.

Deng, through his successes in the real world, understands this challenge of collaboration, as we can see in the wisdom from his lecture at Uppsala University as UN Secretary General Special Adviser for the Prevention of Genocide in which he said,"...we [idealists] might cry out loud, stand on the mountain-top and preach what is right and condemn what is wrong. However, when we do that, we might satisfy our conscience, but how much can we help the people who need to be helped in a practical way".

6. Conclusion

The African village has long been envisioned as an ideal oasis of pristine organization amidst the turbulence of modernity as represented by the city, with all its promises and woes. However, there may also be some things more immediately relevant in how the African village was designed, in harmony and balance with the natural and human diversities that constitute the ecosystem in which the concept of a village is embedded. For unlike the city, the village is part of a natural landscape, including not only its structures that blend seamlessly, but also its governance, whose symbol is the tree, under which members of community sit to discuss.

Deng's inner identification with his maternal lineage established the moral core at the heart of the Invisible Bridge and is the spiritual grounding that connects him back to his identity as a Ngok Dinka. While his skill as a diplomat comes from his identification with the court of his father, Deng Majok, the more basic architecture of his moral thought arguably comes from his mother and her line, including his persuasive conciliatory tendency to reach out. These two lines interplay synergistically to complement one another in giving weight to the spiritual consequences of actions, enmeshed by idealism, and to the art of diplomacy and administration, enmeshed in realism. Indeed, this is the theme of Deng's upcoming book, *Blood of Two Streams:*

Legacies of Paternal and Maternal Lineages.

Deng's ideas suggest that knowing oneself deeply and having the inner perspective to see the universal foundations of one's identity allow one to make linkages to other people. As he travelled, Deng sees the core values of his own African culture not as primitive and backwards, to be left behind, but as a positive enrichment. He was able to see the universalizing elements of where he came from and how it feeds into the world he went into, thus allowing him to see the integration of worlds. He took this perspective to the national and global levels before returning to his home country after his UN service.

Whereas many have left the village with ambivalence about being from a primitive culture, Deng was not ashamed of where he came from or even his father's polygyny. Rather, he used it as a platform that he puts boldly on the table, to analyze, discuss and be proud of, while also realizing its limits and the imperatives of change. In this sense, the invisible bridge has to do with the way you know yourself as well as reach out to others. Without, however, a concerted process of introspection, self-knowledge may be elusive, and external relations weak.

While not explicitly cultivating the village concept through his voluminous empirical work early in his academic career, Deng's overall worldview is rooted in his early work and based on a deconstruction of the idea of an African village including analysis of songs, folktales, hymns, myths, and interviews of all elements of Dinka sociology and culture and their reconstruction. It is in his exploration of his own people, from a perspective deep within his father's court, his mother's homestead, and his community's cattle byres, that Deng roots an integral worldview that he has articulated locally, nationally, continentally and globally, using different formulations, all expressing the same basic structure – that humans though constituted of various component parts, taken from maternal and paternal contributions, are nonetheless whole, and their various levels of administration, starting with their own physical maintenance and presentation, should be a reflection of such wholeness, which he finds in the notion of human dignity.

While rooted internally in the reconciliation of his maternal and paternal lines, representing administrative and moral order respectively, Deng's bridging concept took shape as an expression of his father's attempt to manage relations internally within a large extended family at the heart of the Ngok Dinka, across borders with neighboring communities and particularly the Missiriya Arabs to the north, and with the government(s) of northern and southern Sudan. These differences, and the need to bridge them, remain as challenging as ever, and Deng has not given up his belief that such a bridge is possible.

About the Authors

Daniel J. Deng is a Principal Development Practice Specialist at Development Alternatives International's (DAI's) Center for Secure and Stable States. He has 20-years of experience in strategic planning and execution of development activities across Africa where he has worked within Government ministries, UN agencies, private sector companies and non-governmental organizations. He has led teams and developed organizational design and workflow processes across a dozen African countries. After receiving his bachelor's degree from the University of

Pennsylvania in Urban Studies, Deng traveled extensively across Africa, Asia and Europe facilitating collaboration across government, business and non-governmental sectors. In the process, he continued his post-graduate studies at the University of South Africa (UNISA) Center for African Renaissance Studies and the University of Juba Institute for Peace, Development and Security Studies where he researched on the application of social contract theory to Africa. Deng has a natural belief in development and that sustainable technologies can reinforce universal values and build local economies. He is committed to seeing development cooperation become a more effective mechanism for achieving greater harmony and balance among people(s) and with nature.

 **Luka Kuol (PhD)** is a Professor at Africa Center for Strategic Studies (ACSS), National Defense University, US. He is also Associate Professor of Economics at University of Juba and a Global Fellow at Peace Research Institute Oslo (PRIO), Norway. He was resident fellow at Harvard Kennedy School, former director of Center for Peace and Development Studies at University of Juba and academic staff at University of Gezira, Sudan. He served as a minister of presidency of Southern Sudan and as a National Minister of Cabinet Affairs of Sudan during the Sudan Comprehensive Peace Agreement until he resigned in 2011. He also worked as a Senior Economist for the World Bank in Southern Sudan and a founding member of

Daniel Deng & Luka Kuol

New Sudan Center for Statistics and Evaluation (currently South Sudan National Bureau of Statistics). He received his PhD from the Institute of Development Studies (IDS) at University of Sussex, UK and earned a Master of Arts in Economics and a Master of Business Administration (MBA) from the Catholic University of Leuven, Belgium and Bachelor of Science (Honors) from Faculty of Economics and Social Sciences, University of Khartoum, Sudan. He has published scholarly articles in a wide array of international journals and contributed with many peer-reviewed chapters in various books. His most recent research products include report by the World Food Program (WFP) entitled *"At the Root of Exodus: Food security, conflict and international migration"*, report by United Nations Evaluation Group (UNEG) entitled *"The Humanitarian – Development Nexus: What do evaluations say about it?"*, and report by United Nations Development Program

(UNDP) entitled *"Forging Resilient Social Contracts: A Pathway to Preventing Violent Conflict and Sustaining Peace"*. He is a co-editor of book entitled "The Struggle for South Sudan: Challenges of Security and State Formation".